The Extraordinary Book of Science Experiments that Save the Planet

Written by Helen Bell
Illustrated by Bethan Richards

CUT OUT and MAKE the PROJECTS.
SAVE the INSTRUCTION STRIPS for your
SCIENCE EXPERIMENTS HANDBOOK.

A message from Helen Bell,
a university lecturer who makes science fun

Welcome, planet protectors!

Science is an exciting way to explore and find out about the world around us. It's all about looking at things closely, experimenting, and testing out new ideas. Scientists use their discoveries to find answers to problems and make positive changes all around the world.

Science can inspire new inventions or come up with better ways of doing things. Just look at renewable energy—wind turbines, solar-powered homes, and electric cars were all made possible through scientific discoveries. Science has found cures for illnesses, created artificial intelligence, and made space exploration happen!

One of the biggest problems scientists are working to solve today is climate change. The Earth is getting warmer, which is affecting people, plants, and animals. But don't worry—there are lots of things we can all do!

In this book, you'll learn about some of the causes of climate change and find out what you can do to help take care of the planet! The best part? You'll get to do some fun experiments along the way.

Each experiment comes with a template that you can cut, fold, and stick together to make something you'll need to use. You will also need some common household items, so make sure you have everything on hand before you get started. Tear out and keep the instruction strips so you can do the experiments again whenever you want!

Use your skills to protect the planet through science!

Helen has been a teacher for over twenty years and has enjoyed teaching practical science to children of all ages in lots of different schools. That's a lot of exciting experiments! She is now a lecturer in primary education at Sheffield Hallam University and trains new teachers to make science fun and engaging for the children in their classes.

Helen Bell

CONTENTS

1 **Make it rain** by creating a water cycle
2 **Move a train** using magnetic power
3 **Make a pollinator** and learn how flowers grow
4 **Test the Sun** by exposing paper to UV rays
5 **Race fluids** to see how quickly they can spread
6 **Test paper strength** by using it as a tool
7 **Make a chamber** to watch woodlice choose a habitat
8 **Grow vegetables** from scraps to reduce food waste
9 **Make a strong slope** to protect buildings from landslides
10 **Move a hovercraft** with a puff of air
11 **Launch a fizzy rocket** by exploring chemical reactions
12 **Observe balance** in a rainforest ecosystem
13 **Cook with sunshine** by making a solar oven
14 **Gaze at the stars** to investigate light pollution
15 **Go chemical-free** with an Earth-friendly cleaner
16 **Shake it up** by building a seismograph
17 **Color a picture** using natural dyes
18 **Bury garbage** to see what biodegrades
19 **Use a banana** to learn how to feed plants with peels
20 **Explore wind power** by making bath boats
21 **Clean water** using a filtration system
22 **Paint with leaves** by extracting chlorophyll
23 **Make packaging** from recycled paper
24 **Use soap power** to test how germs are repelled
25 **Catch fish** with responsible methods
26 **Watch sea levels rise** and observe changing habitats
27 **Dig for fuel** to investigate fossil fuel mining
28 **Map food miles** to help the environment
29 **Predict the weather** by making a barometer
30 **Stop heat escaping** by testing insulation

MAKE IT RAIN
by creating a water cycle

1 Make a water cycle in a bag.

The Sun shines on the water in our lakes and seas and heats it up, turning it into water vapor. This process is called evaporation.

Water vapor rises into the sky to form clouds. When the vapor cools down, it becomes liquid again in a process called condensation.

Rain, snow, hail, or sleet falls back down to Earth. This is called precipitation.

Can you make a water cycle using a plastic bag and a warm window?

Water Cycle

You will need

Half a glass of water

Sealable plastic bag

Adhesive tape

Scissors

Blue food coloring

Water cycle symbols on next page

Pour water and blue food coloring into a sealable plastic bag to create an inch-high "pool."

2 Make sure the bag is sealed tight and tape it to a window facing the Sun.

Cut out and stick these pieces on or above the plastic bag to create your very own water cycle.

Cut out all the pieces.

Did you know?
The water cycle is important to keep the Earth at a healthy temperature. Without it, the Earth would be too hot or too cold for us to live on!

Condensation

Precipitation

Evaporation

3 Cut out the water cycle symbols.

4 Attach the symbols, keywords, and arrows to the bag to explain the cycle.

5 Watch evaporation, condensation, and precipitation happen before your eyes!

Protect our planet!
You can help save water in your home by:

Turning taps off when not in use.

Collecting rainwater to water plants.

Taking shorter showers!

MOVE A TRAIN
using magnetic power

2 Watch magnetic force in action.

Magnets produce invisible forces that pull some metals toward them (this is called attracting) and push other metals away (also know as repelling).

Maglev trains are amazing trains that run on magnets!

Strong magnets repel each other so that the train can hover above the track. Different magnets attract the train, propelling it forward.

Magnet maze

You will need

Maze and train on next page

Paper clip

Adhesive tape

Scissors

Fridge magnet

1 Carefully cut out the maze and train.

2 Stick a paper clip to the front of the train with some adhesive tape.

Test magnetic attraction to complete the maze.

Take your magnet on a mission to find magnetic materials in your home. Are all metals magnetic?

Maglev Station

Start

Protect our planet!

Maglev trains waste less energy than other modes of transportation.

Maglev trains don't use fossil fuels like other vehicles, such as cars.

What other forms of transportation are environmentally friendly?

3 Put the train on the start of the maze with the paper clip facing down.

4 Position your magnet underneath the train on the other side of the paper.

5 Using the fridge magnet, see if you can guide the train along the maze.

MAKE A POLLINATOR
and learn how flowers grow

3 Discover how pollination works.

Bees move pollen from one flower to another. This process is called pollination, and it's vital for the survival of life on Earth.

When a bee lands on a flower, a special dust called pollen sticks to its body.

Bees fly from flower to flower to collect sweet nectar.

The bee travels to another flower and some pollen drops off.

The flower uses the new pollen to make seeds and grow new plants.

There are thousands of kinds of pollinating insects. The pollen they spread is needed to make new plants grow. Without them, many crops would die out and humans and other animals would run out of food.

A pollinating bee

You will need

Adhesive tape

Scissors

Bee and flowers on next page

2 plates

Flour

Brown sugar

Popsicle stick

1. Cut out the bee and two flowers. Put each flower on a clean plate.

2. Stick the popsicle stick underneath the bee with adhesive tape.

How do you think you can move pollen from one flower to another?

Cut out all the pieces.

Did you know?

Honeybees can visit up to 5,000 flowers in one day! They pollinate crops that provide us with delicious fruits such as blueberries, cucumbers, and apples. Thank you, honeybees!

3 Double over pieces of adhesive tape and stick underneath the bee's wings.

4 Add sugar to the center of one flower and flour to the other. Pretend the sugar is pollen!

5 What happens when the bee lands on the brown sugar, then lands on the flour?

Protect our planet!

Make your garden a bee-friendly place!

Plant some bee-friendly plants.

Don't use harmful chemicals in the garden.

Put stones in shallow water to make a bee bath!

TEST THE SUN
by exposing paper to UV rays

4 Test the strength of the Sun's rays.

Ultraviolet (UV) rays are natural energy produced by the Sun. These can be damaging to skin. Can you test the strength of UV rays on paper?

We use sunscreen to absorb some of the UV rays from the Sun to protect our skin.

Sunscreen picture

You will need

Scissors | Sun on next page

Black construction paper | Sticky putty

1 Cut out the Sun to create a stencil.

2 Stick it to black kraft paper with small bits of sticky putty so it's as flat as possible.

Cut out all the blue pieces.

Protect our planet!

You can protect yourself and others from the Sun!

3. Stick your picture to a window that gets lots of sunshine, with the Sun facing out.

4. Take down your picture every few days and look at how it has changed.

5. Is there a difference between the covered black paper and paper exposed to the Sun?

Move to a shaded space during the hottest part of the day.

Use a high-factor sunscreen (SPF 50).

Wear a T-shirt, hat, and sunglasses to protect your skin and eyes.

RACE FLUIDS
to see how quickly they can spread

5 Compare how fast fluids spread.

Fluids are substances that can flow and can take the shape of their container. When they are not contained, they can spread.

Cargo ships carrying fluids sometimes have accidents. What do you think happens if fluids spill into the ocean? Which fluid do you think will spread the fastest in this experiment?

Racetrack

You will need

Water, Cooking oil, Ketchup, Honey, Teaspoon, Stopwatch or timer

1. Cut out the racetrack.

Racetrack on next page

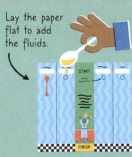

Lay the paper flat to add the fluids.

2. Add half a teaspoon of each fluid at the starting position.

TEST PAPER STRENGTH
by using it as a tool

6 Make a strong tool using paper.

Think scientifically by challenging how things work. Can we look at different ways to use everyday materials?

Paper knives

You will need

Cucumber slice half an inch thick

Adhesive tape

Scissors

Peeled banana (or a strawberry if you don't like bananas)

Paper strips on next page

1 Cut out the paper strips.

2 Hold strip A at both ends and stretch it tight. Can it chop the banana?

Cut out two paper knives to chop up your snacks!

Strip A

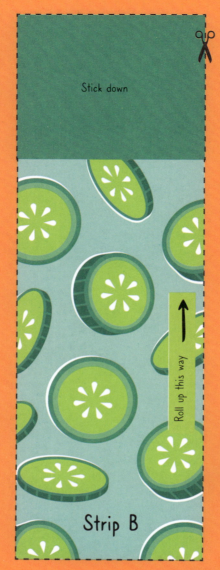

Stick down

Roll up this way

Strip B

Did you know?

The structure of paper affects its strength. In the experiment, did both shapes work on the hard cucumber? Which was stronger, the straight paper or the tube of paper?

What happened?
Did both shapes work on the hard cucumber?

3. Now try chopping the cucumber. What happens?

4. Roll strip B and stick together with some tape to make a tube.

5. Try chopping the cucumber with the tube. What happens?

Protect our planet!

Be resourceful! Sometimes we don't have the tools that we need for a job. Always look for ways to get things done with the resources you have available to you!

MAKE A CHAMBER
to watch woodlice choose a habitat

7
Set up a choice chamber for woodlice.

Woodlice are super composters that feed on dead leaves and plants. What kind of habitat do they need to survive?

Choice chamber

You will need

3–4 woodlice—collect these carefully outside and put back in the place you found them

Adhesive tape

Scissors

Chamber on next page

Soil, leaves, stones, bark, and twigs

1 Cut out the chamber template and stick the corners together.

2 Sprinkle a thin layer of soil on the bottom of the tray and spray with a little water.

Cut off corner tab

A B

Fold up sides

Fold up sides

Fold up sides

Fold up sides

Cut off corner tab

Cut off corner tab

Cut off corner tab

Guess which habitat the woodlice choose.

3 On side A, create a shelter by gently covering with leaves, moss, bark, and sticks.

4 Leave side B with just soil. Find 3 to 4 woodlice and carefully put them on side B.

5 Do the woodlice stay on side B? What does that tell you about the habitats they prefer?

Protect our planet!

Extreme weather such as high rainfall or heat can threaten habitats. Woodlice prefer cool temperatures and moist environments, which they use as a safe space to lay their eggs and hide from predators. Can you make a bug-friendly zone at home or at school?

GROW VEGETABLES
from scraps to reduce food waste

8 Watch a veggie scrap grow.

We can help protect the planet by growing vegetables from scraps and reducing the amount of food waste we throw away.

Vegetable scraps with roots or leaves can keep growing if you put them in water.

Can you grow a spring onion scrap in water? Look for the ends of spring onions with roots showing. What do you think will happen?

Eating lots of vegetables is a great way to keep your body healthy. Eating more vegetables and less meat is also good for the planet.

Growth chart

You will need

Some spring onion scraps with roots showing

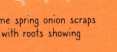
Growth chart on next page

Adhesive tape

Scissors

Jar

Rubber band

1 Take some 2-inch-high spring onion scraps. Secure them with a rubber band.

2 Put them in a glass jar (with the root end facing down). Add water.

Measure how tall the spring onion grows.

cm
18 17 16 15 14 13 12 11 10 9 8 7 6 5 4 3 2 1

Cut these out to stick on the fridge!

Protect our planet!

Eat more vegetables

Save our scraps!

Stick down

Use this green strip to make a hook for your chart.

3 Cut out the height chart. Stick on the hook and hook it over your jar.

4 Wait a few days to see what happens. Can you guess how tall it will grow?

5 The new spring onion is edible, but you can pot it in soil to see if it flowers!

Protect our planet!

Go vegetarian one day a week. Try meat-free Mondays!

Growing your own vegetables is much better for the environment than buying your vegetables from a supermarket.

MAKE A STRONG SLOPE
to protect buildings from landslides

9 Test landslide defenses.

Heavy rain can be a cause of landslides. When landslides happen, they can strike quickly and are very dangerous.

Logging, or cutting down trees, can make slopes weaker.

Scientists work out ways to prevent landslides by making slopes stronger.

Landslide model

You will need

Slopes and houses on next page

Adhesive tape

Tray

Uncooked rice

Sticky putty

Scissors

1 Cut out and fold two slopes. Fold and stick together two houses.

2 On slope B, stick six small balls of sticky putty on the black dots. Imagine these are trees.

Slide A ✂   Slide B ✂   Make two little houses.

Fold here   Fold here   Fold here   Fold here

Cut these out to make two houses to position at the bottom of each slope.

✂
Fold ✂ Fold ✂
Fold   Fold
Fold   Fold
✂
Fold ✂ Fold

Protect our planet!
Engineering is a science. Engineers investigate ways to protect the environment.

3 Tape the bottom of each slope to the tray and put a house at the bottom of each.

4 Pour a teaspoon of rice at the top of each slope. Tip the slopes up the same height.

5 What happened? Did the sticky putty trees affect how much rice slid down the slope?

They start by building models to look at possible landslide damage.

Think like an engineer. What else could you do to stop landslide damage?

MOVE A HOVERCRAFT
with a puff of air

10 Observe lift with a paper model.

A hovercraft is able to travel over water, land, mud, and ice. Powerful fans create a cushion of air that is trapped beneath the vehicle and creates lift, which moves the craft up.

Propellers push air backward and create thrust to move the vehicle forward.

lift

air movement

The air pressure above the vehicle is lower than the pressure below and this creates lift!

Paper hovercraft

1. Cut out the template and fold the paper in half, diagonally.

2. Fold this triangle in half again to make a smaller triangle.

3. Unfold the triangle and turn the paper over.

4. Fold up each side to the middle to make a kite shape.

Fold along this dotted line to begin.

Create stronger air currents using a balloon pump, a fan, or even a hair dryer to power your hovercraft!

5 Fold the two middle edges out to the edge of the kite shape.

6 Flip your hovercraft over.

7 Put your hovercraft on a flat surface. Pull the fins outward.

8 Where do you think you need to direct air to make your hovercraft move?

Protect our planet!

Hovercrafts are more environmentally friendly th boats because they hover above the surface, causing very little disturbance to water and marine life.

LAUNCH A FIZZY ROCKET
by exploring chemical reactions

11
Create gas and blast off a rocket.

When a rocket is launched, it releases a large amount of carbon dioxide (CO_2) gas into the atmosphere.

Too much CO_2 is warming up the planet. Aerospace engineers are looking for ways to reduce CO_2 emissions by testing alternative, greener fuels such as hydrogen.

Fizzy rocket

You will need

Rocket on next page

Scissors

Adhesive tape

Tray

Tube of fizzy vitamin tablets (remove the tablets)

Safety goggles

Water

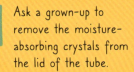
1 Ask a grown-up to remove the moisture-absorbing crystals from the lid of the tube.

2 Cut out the rocket and stick it to the empty tube, with the hole at the bottom of the rocket.

Cut out the rocket and prepare for launch.

Did you know?

The gas in soft drinks is also CO_2. Shaking a closed soft drink bottle makes the bubbles grow and push liquid out of the way, causing a frothy explosion!

CO_2 builds inside the tube and the pressure forces the lid off! The tube is thrust into the air just like a rocket being launched.

Protect our planet!

3 Pour 2 inches of water in the tube.

4 Put half a vitamin tablet into the lid and put on your safety goggles.

5 Put the lid onto the tube securely, turn it upside down, and stand back!

Lots of motor vehicles produce CO_2. Next time you are on a bus, think about how many cars would be on the road if everyone on the bus had chosen to drive. Buses are greener!

OBSERVE BALANCE
in a rainforest ecosystem

12 Learn about the importance of balance.

South America's Amazon rainforest is home to thousands of species of plants and animals that need each other to survive.

Herbivores, omnivores, and carnivores depend on trees, plants, and even each other for food, shelter, and protection.

Decomposers are animals and plants that help keep the ground full of nutrients.

Ecosystem balancer

You will need

Animals and plants on next page

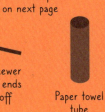
Bamboo skewer with sharp ends snipped off · Paper towel tube

Paper clips

Scissors

Adhesive tape

1 Cut out the plants and animals.

2 Tape an opened paper clip to the back of each shape to make a hook.

Cut out these rainforest plants and animals.

3 Flatten one end of the tube and tape it closed. Balance the skewer on the notch.

Cut a V-shaped notch in the center.

Balance is about making things level.

4 Hook on all the things that depend on each other in the rainforest. Can you make it balance?

5 Pretend you are a logging company and remove a tree. What happens?

Protect our planet!

Areas of rainforest are being cleared by humans every year. Destroying this habitat threatens the survival of many animals. Here's what you can do to help:

Reduce, reuse, and recycle paper.

Eat less meat.

Adopt a rainforest animal.

COOK WITH SUNSHINE
by making a solar oven

13 Use renewable energy to make a snack.

Renewable energy is energy that nature can replace, so it will never run out. Can you use sunlight (solar energy) to cook food?

Solar oven

You will need

Black construction paper

Cardboard box (with taped-up sides)

Graham crackers

Plastic wrap

Scissors

Adhesive tape

Aluminum foil

Marshmallows

Chocolate

1 Cut a flap in the top of the box, then tape aluminum foil to the inner side of it.

2 Line the inside of the box with black paper. Cover the box window with plastic wrap and tape in place.

How to make S'MORES

First, gather your ingredients.

You will need:
1 marshmallow
2 graham crackers
1 square of chocolate

Next, melt a marshmallow in your solar oven. While it is melting, put two graham crackers, and a square of chocolate on a plate.

Now, build your s'more! Put a melted marshmallow on a graham cracker, add a square of chocolate, and top with the other cracker.

4 Position the box so the flap reflects the Sun into the oven. Wait 15 minutes.

Prop open the flap with a twig.

5 Put a marshmallow inside the oven and a second outside the oven. Wait an hour.

Which marshmallow melted?

6 Clip together the recipe booklet to make a yummy s'more.

Protect our planet!

Solar ovens can be very useful in areas without electricity.

Solar ovens are lightweight, so they're great for camping or for taking on picnics.

Alternative energy solutions are better for the environment!

GAZE AT THE STARS
to investigate light pollution

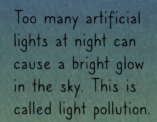
14 Test the effect of artificial lights.

City lights make it safe for humans at night but are not good for animals that rely on the dark to survive.

Too many artificial lights at night can cause a bright glow in the sky. This is called light pollution.

Star projector

You will need

Cell phone with the flashlight switched on

Projector templates on next page

Pencil and modeling clay

Adhesive tape

Scissors

1 Cut out the templates. Fold the long template into a tube and stick together with tape.

2 Press the disc against some modeling clay and poke some holes in it with a pencil.

Cut out and stick together a star projector.

Project stars onto your ceiling and experiment with the effects of light pollution.

3. Lay a cell phone on a table. Balance the projector over the flashlight.

4. Close the door and switch off the room light to look at the stars on the ceiling.

5. Open a door to introduce light. What happens to the stars?

Protect our planet!
You can help reduce light pollution.

Turn out lights when they aren't needed.

Use warm-colored LED bulbs.

Use outdoor lights with shie that direct ligh downward.

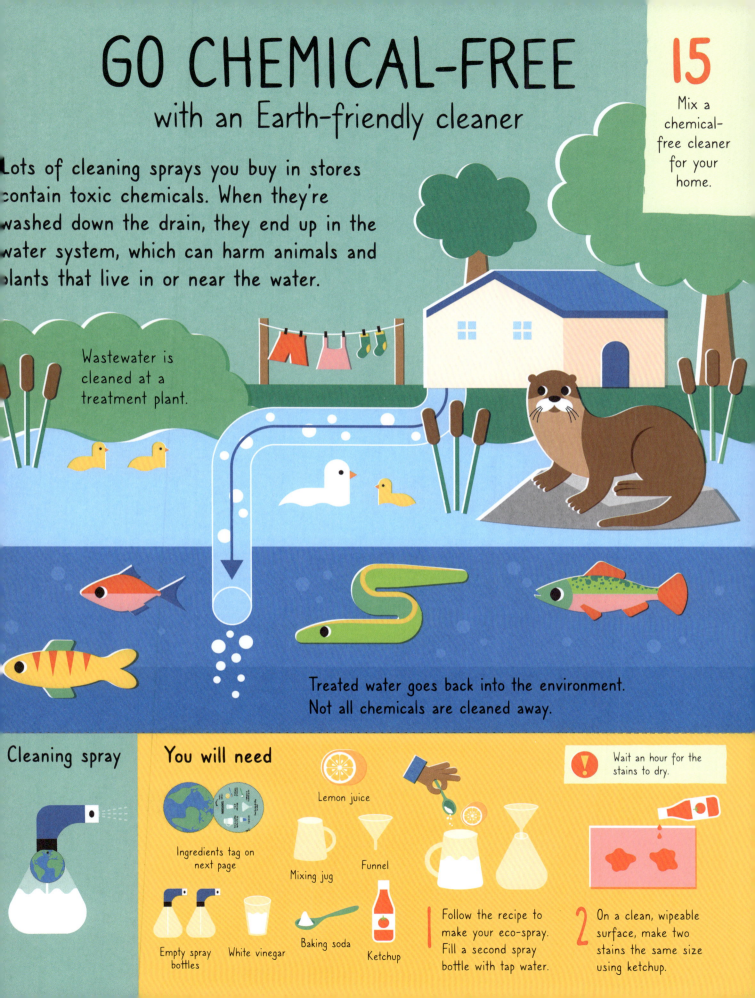

Cut out a tag to hang around your bottle. Use it again and again!

Vinegar is an acid that breaks down dirt and disinfects surfaces.

Baking soda scrubs away dirt and absorbs smells.

Water dilutes the mixture, making it safe for use on various surfaces and allowing it to cover more area.

Lemon juice makes it smell good!

Did you know?
When vinegar and baking soda combine, they react to produce bubbles of carbon dioxide gas, creating a fizzing action that helps remove dirt.

Fold along the dotted line.

Punch a hole here.

INGREDIENTS
- 1 cup of white vinegar
- 1 cup of water
- 2 tablespoons lemon juice
- 1 tablespoon of baking soda

METHOD
Mix all the ingredients together in a jug.

Use a funnel to pour your eco-spray into a bottle.

3 Spray one stain with three squirts of eco-spray and the other with three squirts of water.

4 Wait a few minutes. Can you see the eco-spray start to break down the dirt?

5 Which stain was cleaned best? Test the eco-spray on other food stains.

Protect our planet!

Take your shoes off when you get home. Your shoes pick up lots of dirt and germs outside.

Grow indoor plants like jasmine or roses for natural air fresheners.

SHAKE IT UP
by building a seismograph

16 Measure the strength of an earthquake.

Scientists use seismographs to measure how strong earthquakes are and to try to understand them better.

The Earth's surface is made up of plates that fit together like jigsaw pieces. When they rub against each other, they shake.

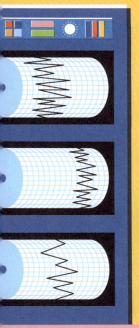

The shaking plates cause vibrations that travel like waves through the Earth's surface. These can be read by a seismograph.

Seismograph

You will need

- Small cardboard box with no lid
- 2 rubber bands cut in half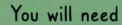
- Coins
- Adhesive tape
- Scissors
- Paper cup
- Pen

1 Make two holes in the top of the box and two 3-inch slits at the bottom on opposite sides.

2 Make two holes in the cup. Hang the cup from the holes at the top using the rubber bands.

Tape these strips together to feed into your seismograph.

Make the slots at the bottom of the box 3 inches long.

 Make a hole in the bottom of the cup and poke the pen through.

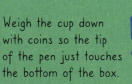 Weigh the cup down with coins so the tip of the pen just touches the bottom of the box.

5 Pass the strips of paper through the slots while shaking your box. Can you read the waves?

Gently shake your box!

Protect our planet!

Engineers design strong buildings in areas at risk of earthquakes to prevent them from falling down.

Make buildings of different shapes from construction blocks. Make some tall, thin, short, and wide. Which do you think will stand up in an earthquake?

COLOR A PICTURE
using natural dyes

17 Make colored paint from plants.

Natural dyes are colors that come from pigments in plants, animals, or minerals. Natural dyes can be used to color food, fabrics, cosmetics, and art materials.

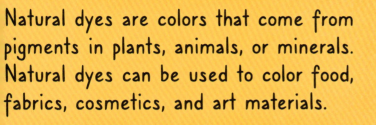

Natural dyes are much better for our planet than manufactured dyes and paint, which can contain toxins.

Painted picture

You will need

3 small bowls

Cotton swabs or paintbrushes

Ground turmeric

Pan of water

1 medium-sized beet

Spoons for mixing

 Ask a grown-up to help with chopping and heating.

1 Chop up the beet and add to a saucepan. Cover up with water.

2 Bring to a boil then turn the heat down to simmer. What do you notice about the water?

Paint this picture using the natural dye you've made.

Did you know?

People in ancient Egypt, China, and the Americas used plants, minerals, and insects to create beautiful colors.

Be careful—beet and turmeric stain!

4 Leave to cool, then ask an adult to drain the liquid into a bowl. This is ready to paint with.

5 In a cup, mix 2 teaspoons of turmeric with a little water to a paint consistency.

6 Experiment by painting the picture above. Test the colors on a scrap of old fabric, too.

Protect our planet!

Natural dyes from plants and animals are a renewable resource and won't ever run out! Look for clothing and toys that have been produced using sustainable resources.

BURY GARBAGE
to see what biodegrades

18 — Test which materials biodegrade.

Plastic is a useful material for lots of purposes because it's strong and long-lasting. But sadly, most plastic can't biodegrade like natural materials can.

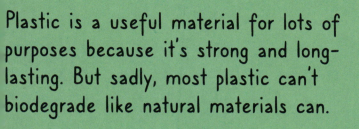

When something is biodegradable, it breaks down and eventually disappears into the Earth. This is nature's way of cleaning up and recycling!

Animals like worms, woodlice, and termites eat rotting matter, then release nutrients back into the soil to help plants stay healthy.

Plastic doesn't break down, meaning it stays in the soil or is eaten by animals, entering the food chain.

Labels

You will need

Garbage labels on next page

Apple core

Popsicle sticks

Leaf

Rubber band

Dish-washing sponge

Adhesive tape

1 Cut out the garbage labels and cover in tape to waterproof. Stick each label to a popsicle stick.

2 Find a space in the ground where you won't damage plants. Dig five small holes.

Cut out these labels and stick to popsicle sticks.

- Apple core
- Sponge
- Green leaf
- Rubber band
- Book paper

Bury this piece and see what happens.

Guess which items will rot and which will not.

Protect our planet!

3 Gather your items, including the test piece of paper from the page above.

4 Put each item in a hole and cover with soil. Use a label to show where each thing is buried.

Put all the items in the trash at the end of the experiment!

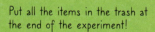

5 Wait two weeks before uncovering your items. Did you guess correctly which would rot?

Use reusable containers and bottles for food and water.

Choose toys made from sustainable materials such as metal, wood, or recycled plastics.

USE A BANANA
to learn how to feed plants with peels

19 Make a natural fertilizer for your houseplants.

Banana peels make excellent plant fertilizers because they contain the essential nutrients needed to enrich the soil without harming the environment.

Banana tea is a natural fertilizer that makes use of food waste!

Banana peels are high in potassium and phosphorus, essential nutrients for growing healthy plants.

Banana Boost

You will need

- Banana skins
- Popsicle stick
- Labels on next page

- Recycled plastic bottle
- 2 small indoor potted plants the same size
- Adhesive tape
- Scissors

1 Cut out the banana label and tape it on the plastic bottle with a lid. Cut up some banana skins and put them in the bottle.

2 Top the bottle up with water and put the lid on. Leave to stand for three to seven days.

Label your fertilizer and your pot.

Banana Boost

Natural Fertilizer!

Made by _____

Ingredients: banana skins and water

Nutritious and naturally strong!

Cut out this label and stick it on the bottle.

Cut this out and stick it to one end of a popsicle stick.

Did you know?
In farming, chemical fertilizers can help plants grow but are not healthy for the soil or environment.

3 Take two plants. Cut out the monkey label and tape it to a popsicle stick. Push it into one pot.

4 For a few weeks, water the labeled pot with banana boost and the other with water.

5 Can you see a difference in the two plants? Try it on other plants.

Protect our planet!
Recycle more kitchen scraps in a lidded bucket to add to an outdoor compost heap.

Great foods for composting are chopped fruit and vegetable scraps, coffee grounds, and used tea bags! Avoid composting meat, dairy foods, or foods that are rich in oil.

EXPLORE WIND POWER
by making bath boats

20 Make a boat from card and cork.

Wind energy produces no emissions so can't cause pollution. It is also a renewable energy source so will never run out! Scientists look for the best ways to harness wind energy.

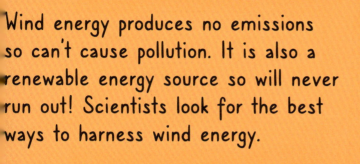

Different sail shapes can harness the wind in different ways, making the boat move faster or slower.

Bath boats

You will need

- 6 rubber bands
- Sails on next page
- 9 corks
- 3 wooden skewers
- Scissors
- Adhesive tape

1. Ask an adult to cut three wooden skewers to 4 inches long.

2. Make three boats by joining three corks in a row using two rubber bands.

Cut out and test these sails.

Make some model boats and test different sail shapes to see which one works best.

3 Stick the pointed end of each skewer into the middle of each boat to make a mast.

4 Attach the sails to the masts with tape and float them in a tub full of water.

5 Can you move the boats with wind energy? Which sail works best?

Protect our planet!
Have lots of fun experimenting with wind.

Fly a kite on a windy day.

Make a wind-powered car with a mast and sail.

Hang up a homemade wind chime outside.

CLEAN WATER
using a filtration system

21 Remove dirt from water.

We need to drink water every day to stay hydrated. Fresh water can be found in rivers, wells, and lakes, but it needs to be filtered to remove dirt and make it clean and safe to drink.

In some countries, where access to clean tap water may be limited, rainwater can be collected, filtered, and stored in tanks for safe drinking.

Water filter

You will need

- Large, empty plastic bottle
- Sticky putty and a pushpin
- Dried herbs
- Jug of tap water
- Gravel or small stones
- Adhesive tape
- Filter on next page

1 Cut a bottle in half and turn the top half upside down to fit it inside the bottom.

2 Cut out the filter. Make lots of tiny holes in the filter using a pushpin with sticky putty underneath.

Put sticky putty under the paper.

Roll and stick into a cone shape.

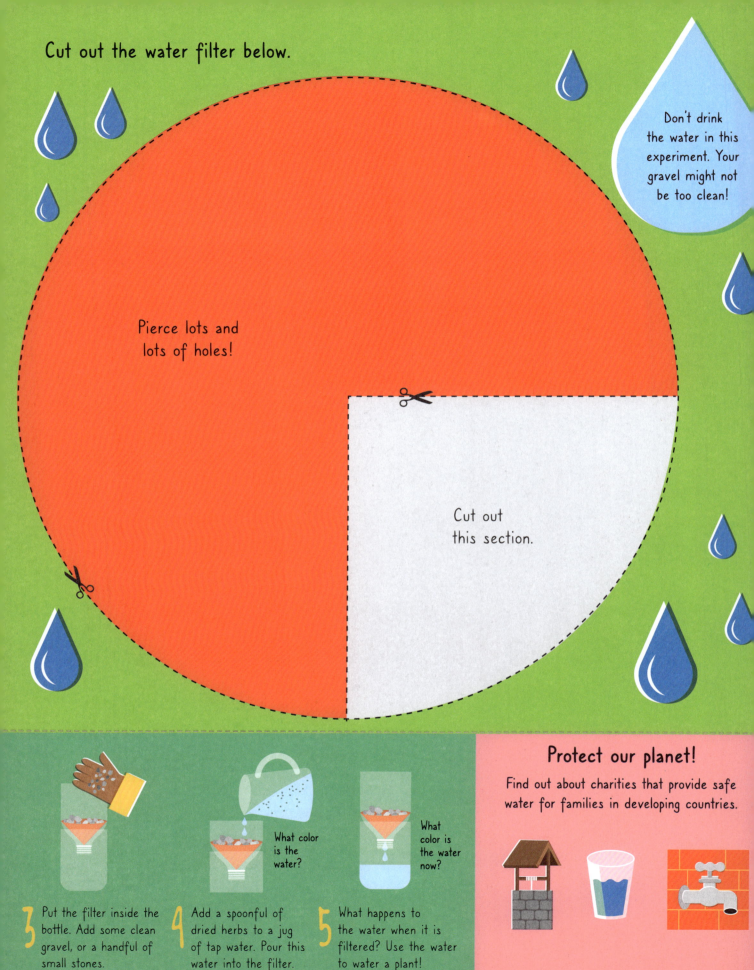

PAINT WITH LEAVES
by extracting chlorophyll

22 Extract the green color from leaves.

Some plants have green leaves because they contain a special green substance called chlorophyll. Chlorophyll absorbs sunlight and turns it into energy to help the plant grow.

The process of turning sunlight into energy is called photosynthesis.

Photosynthesis is essential for life on Earth. Animals depend on plants to survive. Without plants, there would be no animals.

Paper trees

You will need

- 2 glass jars with lids
- Trees on next page
- Fresh green leaves, like spinach or arugula
- Plate
- Alcohol-based hand sanitizer
- Sieve
- Paintbrush

Caution! Keep hand sanitizer away from your face. Dispose of the mixture after use.

1 Tear up some green leaves into smaller bits and put them in one of the jars.

2 Put the jar on a plate and carefully pour hand sanitizer over the leaves. Put on the lid.

Cut out and stand up your tree.

The alcohol in hand sanitizer separates the chlorophyll from the leaves.

3. Let the jar stand for 30 minutes. See if the liquid dissolves the chlorophyll.

4. Strain the chlorophyll into a fresh jar using a sieve or a coffee filter.

5. Cut out the tree model and paint leaves on it. When you have finished, slot it together.

Protect our planet!

Trees produce oxygen, provide homes for anim and help combat climate change by storing car

Help the plants in and around your home by placing them in sunny spots.

Take part in tree-planting events in your community.

Help young trees in your area by water them during weather.

MAKE PACKAGING
from recycled paper

23 Make eco-friendly packaging.

Look in your cabinets and fridge. How many things are packaged in plastic? Plastic packaging can protect some gooey foods, but often, sustainable recycled packaging would work just as well.

Cardboard and paper are a type of material made of wood fibers. These fibers are biogradable but also soak up moisture.

Is cardboard or paper a good packaging choice for all food types?

Snack pack

You will need

Box on next page

Sugar snap peas or dried fruit

Piece of cheese

Plate

Adhesive tape

Half a tomato or cucumber slice

1 Cut out the box and tape together. Fold down the bottom and stick with tape.

2 Put three leftover pieces of cutout book pages on a plate.

Fill your box with snacks to pack in a lunch box.

Glue along here to stick together.

Fold along the dotted lines.

Trace over the orange lines with a ballpoint pen, pressing hard. This will help you fold it later.

3 Take a sample of each food type and rub one of each on the paper cut-outs.

4 Did you guess which foods left a mess and which left the paper clean?

5 Fill up your snack pack with mess-free food and pop it in your lunchbox!

Protect our planet!

Buy loose fruit and vegetables from a produce store, or produce from a supermarket. Pack the items in paper bags. You can find these in the store or bring some from home.

USE SOAP POWER
to test how germs are repelled

24 Watch how soap cleans hands.

Germs are so small, we can't see them, but when you touch your mouth, nose, or eyes, they can get into your body and make you sick.

The soap you use on your hands has ingredients that help repel, or push away, germs. In this experiment, imagine that the pepper is germs. What happens to the germs when using soap?

Paper hands

You will need

 Hands on next page

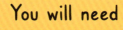 Adhesive tape

 Large shallow bowl

 Soap

 Ground black pepper

4 popsicle sticks

1 Cut out the two pairs of hands. Tape a popsicle stick to the back of each hand.

2 Fill the bowl with water. Sprinkle plenty of pepper to cover the surface.

Hooray for soap!

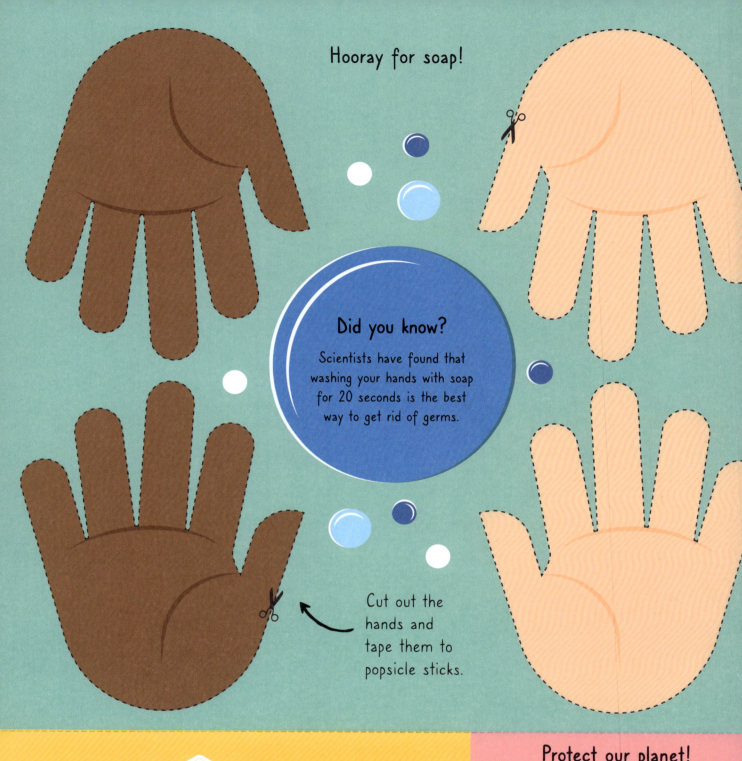

Did you know?
Scientists have found that washing your hands with soap for 20 seconds is the best way to get rid of germs.

Cut out the hands and tape them to popsicle sticks.

3 Dip the fingers of one pair in the water. What happens to the pepper?

4 Gently rub a little soap on the fingers of the other pair. Dip these in the water.

5 What do you notice happens to the pepper, or "germs"?

Protect our planet!
Some soaps are made with plastics or toxic chemicals and are tested on animals.

Look at your packaging. Choose soaps that say they are made with natural products and are cruelty-free.

CATCH FISH
with responsible methods

25 See the effects of overfishing.

Seafood is a good source of protein, and many people rely on fishing to make a living. Overfishing is when people catch fish faster than the fish can reproduce.

Overfishing can cause fish populations to shrink, or even disappear. Catching fewer fish at a time is a more sustainable way of fishing.

If fewer fish are caught in one session, fish left in the water can have babies that replace the numbers of fish caught.

Fishing trawler

You will need

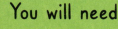
Pasta shapes—these are the fish!

Fishing trawler on next page

Timer

Tablespoon

Adhesive tape

Shallow plastic container—this is the water!

1 Put one mugful of pasta shapes into the container—the fish are now in the water!

UNsustainable fishing

2 Cut out and tape together the fishing trawler. See how many fish you can scoop into the trawler in 30 seconds.

Cut out this fishing trawler. Snip along the lines and fold up and stick together the sides.

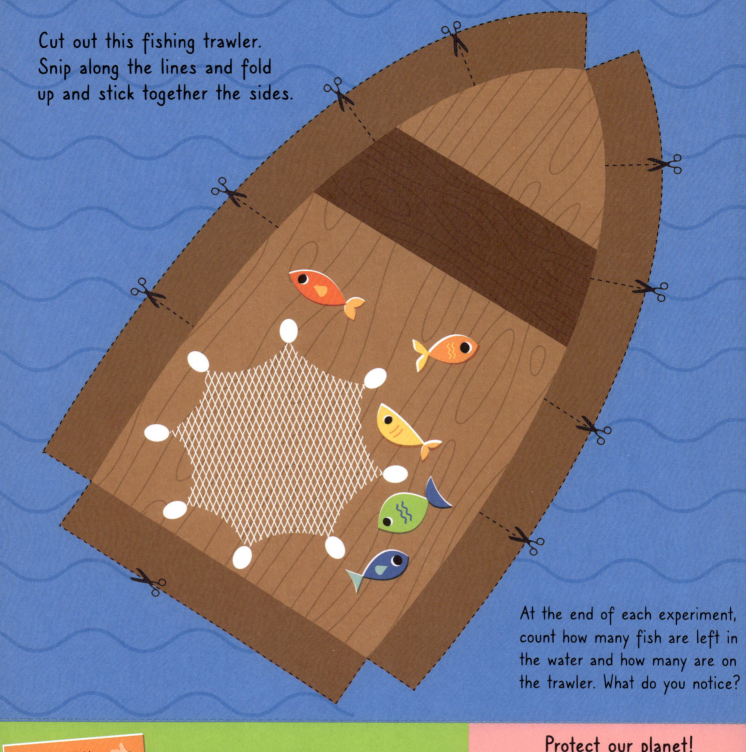

At the end of each experiment, count how many fish are left in the water and how many are on the trawler. What do you notice?

Sustainable fishing

3 Put the fish back in the water. This time, in 30 seconds, catch one fish at a time.

4 Every time you catch a fish, put a new one into the water from the pasta package.

5 What do you notice about the number of fish left in the water and the fish in the trawler?

Protect our planet!
Help promote sustainable fishing.

Choose to buy sustainably sourced fish products. (Check the label.)

Visit a sea-life center to find out more about ocean conservation.

WATCH SEA LEVELS RISE
and observe changing habitats

26 Investigate how sea levels rise.

Polar ice is found either on the frozen land or in the ocean. As the earth warms up, polar ice melts and sea levels rise.

Frozen water on the land is called land ice. Polar bears and other animals live and hunt on the land, in coastal habitats.

Frozen seawater is called sea ice, and floats on the surface of the ocean. Which melting ice—land or sea—destroys coastal habitats?

Polar bears

You will need

- 2 clear plastic containers
- Ice cubes
- Modeling clay
- Sea ice / Land ice — Polar bears and labels on next page
- Ruler
- Adhesive tape
- Marker

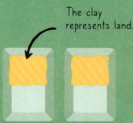

The clay represents land.

1 Cut out the labels. Stick one to each container. Fill up one side of each container with modeling clay.

2 Put six ice cubes in each container as shown to make sea ice and land ice.

Cut out and fold the polar bears.

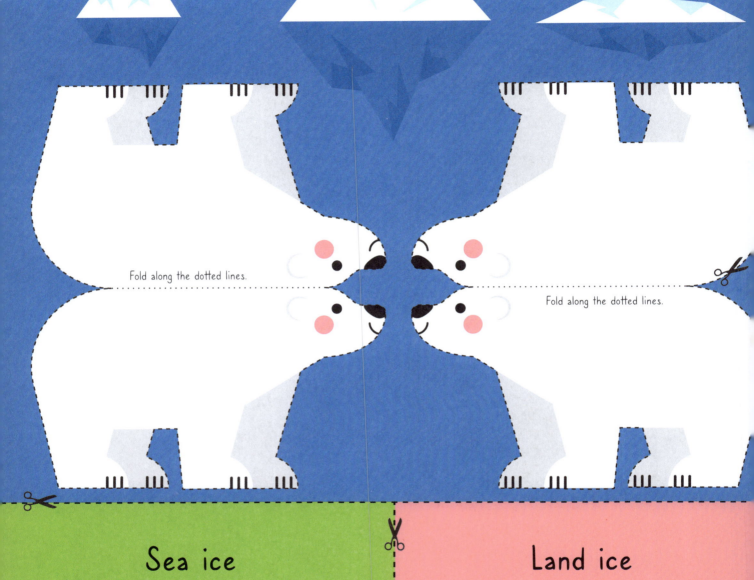

Fold along the dotted lines.

Fold along the dotted lines.

Sea ice

Land ice

Protect our planet!

Frozen coastlines are damaged or destroyed by rising sea levels.

Design a poster about saving polar habitats. Spreading the word about climate change is a really important thing you can do!

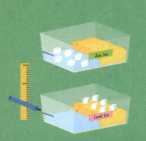

3 Fill both containers with water to just below the land, so the levels match. Mark the levels with a pen.

4 Cut out the polar bears. Balance one bear on the sea ice and one on the land ice. Wait for the ice to melt.

What happens to the sea levels?

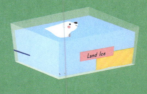

5 Melted land ice adds extra volume to the sea. This makes the sea levels rise.

DIG FOR FUEL
to investigate fossil fuel mining

27 See the effect of mining for fossil fuels.

Fossil fuels are oil, coal, and gas, which are the fossilized remains of plants and animals that died millions of years ago. Lots of the energy we use on Earth is produced by burning fossil fuels.

We get fossil fuels by drilling and mining the Earth, which destroys and pollutes habitats.

Buried fossil fuels

You will need

Chocolate chip cookie

Landscape on next page

Large plate

Toothpicks

1 Cut out the landscape and put it on a large dinner plate.

2 Place a chocolate chip cookie on the page. The cookie represents the untouched habitat.

Cut out the landscape below and place it on your plate.

3 The chocolate chips represent fossil fuels buried deep in the Earth.

4 Holding the cookie in place, dig out the chocolate chips with a toothpick.

5 What happens to the habitat when the fuel is mined?

Protect our planet!

Once fossil fuels are gone, it will take millions of year to replace them.

The Sun, water, and wind are renewable energy sources that will never run out. Scientists investigate new ways to use renewable energy.

MAP FOOD MILES
to help the environment

28 Record the distance your food travels.

Food miles are the distance that food travels from where it's made or grown to your plate. Transporting food across the planet by ships, trains, and planes increases the CO_2 released into the environment.

Some foods lose their nutritional value soon after harvesting. If your food has traveled for many days, it's not as healthy for you.

Chart

You will need

Chart on next page

Pen

Access to a computer

Grown-up to take you to the supermarket

1. Cut out the chart. Visit a supermarket with an adult.

Which food might come from your own country? Can you guess?

2. Try to find all the items on the list. Make a note of the countries of origin.

Record food miles on this chart.  You can find the country of origin, where the food was produced, on a label on the packaging.

Name	Country	Number of miles traveled
Pineapple		
Bananas		
Strawberries		
Loaf of bread		
Chocolate		
Sugar		
Orange juice		

3 When you are at home, look up the distance between each country and your hometown.

4 Write down the number of miles traveled for each item on the chart.

Look for this map at the back of the book!

5 Look at a map to see which food traveled farthest, and which foods are local to you.

Protect our planet!

Find out if any of the food on the chart that traveled from another country can also be grown near your home.

You can reduce food miles by shopping from local farms and buying food that is in season.

PREDICT THE WEATHER
by making a barometer

29 Build a barometer to watch the weather.

The air around us is made up of different gases, like nitrogen, oxygen, and carbon dioxide. These gases are made of tiny molecules that have weight. This weight pushes down on everything around us, and we call that air pressure.

Low pressure

High pressure

"Low pressure" happens when air is rising, making clouds and rainy weather. The lower the pressure, the stormier it is outside!

"High pressure" happens when air is sinking. High pressure means there are fewer clouds and it's likely to be a sunny day!

Barometer

You will need

Empty jar (no lid)

Rubber band

Straw

Glue

Adhesive tape

Balloon

Weather chart on next page

1 Cut away the neck of the balloon and stretch it tightly over the jar. Secure it with a band.

2 Cut the end of the straw into a point. Tape the other end to the middle of the balloon.

Cut out the chart to record the weather.

On warm, sunny days, the air outside the jar is higher pressure than the air trapped inside the jar. Where does the straw point to on the chart as the balloon dips in?

On wet and windy days the air outside the jar is lower pressure than the air trapped inside the jar. See where the straw points now.

3 Cut out the chart and put it next to the jar. Line up the straw with the middle line of the chart, as shown.

4 Put your barometer where the weather is stable, not in direct heat or a draft.

5 Watch the barometer over the next few days. Does it read the weather outside?

Protect our planet!

Understanding weather patterns helps scientists predict when extreme weather events such as hurricanes, floods, or heatwaves will happen.

STOP HEAT ESCAPING
by testing insulation

Humans and animals insulate their homes to stop heat escaping. Choosing the best insulating material for a home is a good way to stop heat loss and use less energy heating homes.

30 Make an insulating box.

Can we save energy by choosing the right insulation?

Insulating box

You will need

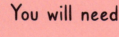
2 ice cubes of the same size

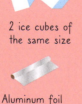
Aluminum foil

Glue

Box on next page

2 small plates

Timer

Small square of bubble wrap

Stick labels to the plates.

1 Cut out and glue together the box. Wrap an ice cube in foil and put it in the box. Close the box lid and put it on plate A.

2 Put the other cube on plate B. Time how long it takes for cube B to melt.

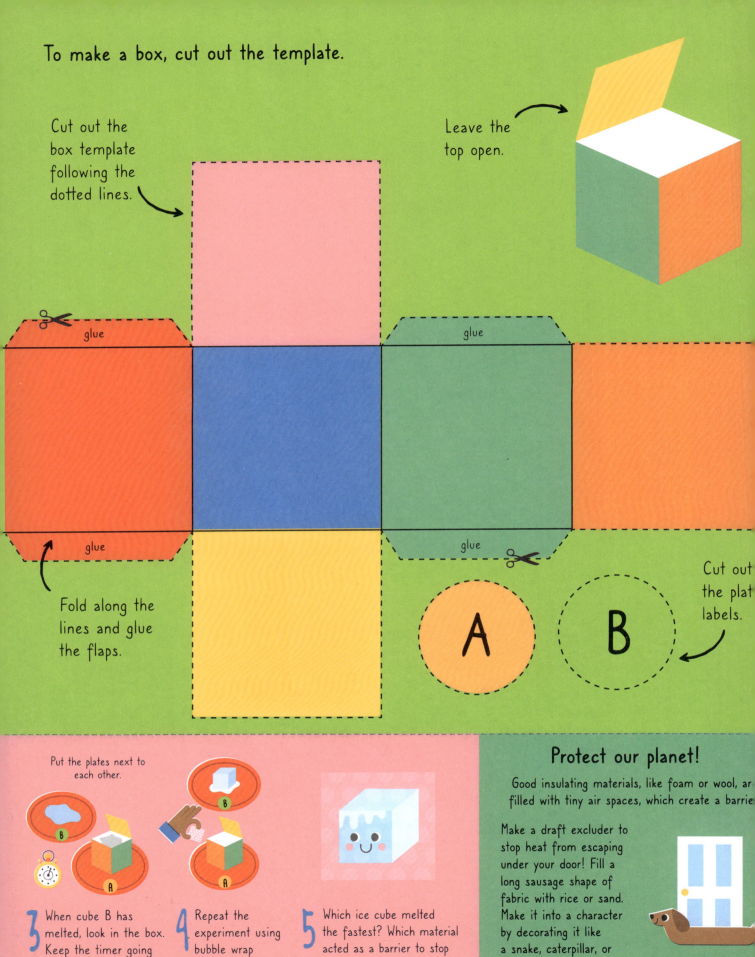